MORALITY PLAY

ALSO BY LAUREN HILGER

Lady Be Good

MORALITY PLAY

poems

LAUREN HILGER

Everett • Seattle
Washington

Cover design by Peter Selgin
Book design by Abi Pollokoff

Poetry NW Editions is an independent, non-profit educational press
in residence at Everett Community College.

LIBRARY OF CONGRESS CONTROL NUMBER: 2022932398
Names: Hilger, Lauren, author
Title: Morality Play / Lauren Hilger
Description: First Edition / Everett, Washington: Poetry NW Editions, 2022
ISBN-13: 978-1-949166-05-7

Poetry NW Editions
2000 Tower Street
Everett, Washington 98201

www.poetrynw.org

CONTENTS

III.

EVEN

I've been still, not moving anything, so when someone walked through the door
and said of the arrangement I had made of myself,
this is exactly how I wanted to find you,
I pretended it was not against nature that it was me—

fresh salt   rerecord   I know how to live my life now.

I love this breeze that messes up my hair,
that whole hall of wind that was always right before
me when I stepped into the gym to perform or try out.
I always imagined a sweet woman who had died before
I was born. I brought her out into that feeling against me.
I imagined her and stepped into it. I imagined it and stepped into it.

That breeze when I had to stomp out of the thorns
in flannel and boots, soft jeans rolled up.

That breeze sitting right up after October sun too long. I'm not made for that.
Made for this inside.
Made on repeat with legs.

That breeze getting out of the Ninth Street Path station, the whole winding staircase,
that whole walk, every petal.

This woman on the street with her eyes closed.
Let this vision stand.
One where I'm patient. One that moves me still.

IN PRAISE OF FOLLY

In Madrid with Erasmus, reading by an open window,

orange trees. Morals.
I had studied for this,

lived under the word *surrender*, had to sing it in a choir.
Born to be a flower girl.

When I said "you" in my diary,
I was trying to reach who'd read it again.

I'd nod before anyone said anything.
Round waved, round mouthed, jewel full of air,

like the female statues in stillness,

uncaressed macrohistorians in a cycle of virtue,
their expression that o,

all swound. We trust what's tranquil.
Wet with grief.

We fell asleep to *Bring It On*. I had just learned to spell lavender.

I wanted the fat yellow pear,
my mom gave me her red heart.

I tried again

by touching the book
until I could feel her touching back.

WHEN YOU KEEP A SECRET LONG ENOUGH, YOU BEGIN TO TELL.

You tell in the way you can tell the handwriting is yours.
There's a difference between this and the rest of knowledge,
where a hand up means stop, a hand up means help me.
When you keep a secret, it becomes an image with a long fuse.
It is bright and ready, the light that is always in your hand. I call out,
I miss you, comrade.
Think of the cruel interior of an early Christian chapel,
not a lot going on in there. It's meant for gold leaf,
framed silences, candle smut.
Melting by the fire, I'm made of that too.
Keep going, no, it's making me sad.
Means I see you. Means there is something before me.

SOUVENIR

        I'd stay up to hold a boy's portrait—
no chain, just the photograph behind glass, half a locket.
I was nine and it was an antique from London that
I'd turn over and back. His face a little pearl,
round witness to the time three towns lost
half their men in a night. It was supposed
to mean, but I couldn't hear it.
A room of rare string instruments behind glass.
But that's the truth, that's the car on which I was
taught brakes. Meaning widened into a field and I'd
have to lie down, the music of this flying through snow.

CERAMIC LAMP WITH CURSIVE MESSAGE

The lamp in the borrowed room said, "This Is It!"
We meant otherwise and the room said no this is it.

There are ways to code intensity on the brain like a map,
like a lamp placed in the kiln, so it could say it

to us. In those rooms unheated and rooms with a fire,
there was an alarm clock going off. I didn't notice. He said it

matches you.
Let's make it

across the river before the bridge falls.
We did. Not frightened by the halo it

gave me, I cracked open the length of my name
to match how long it

would take me to reach you.
The blank moon of a period shortened it.

Each letter a trap door. Like a letter carrier, I found the message
on a torn business envelope. I'd reached for anything when it

came. Silence,
that space inside the envelope. It

was sent before I finished. I meant *I wish I could join you.*
I touch our conversation, it

all disappears. My mother asks, would Lauren Bacall behave
this way? Would she carry on about it?

I say, Ma, this is what happens. This is what happens every time
Schopenhauer uses the Will and I misread it

as love,

—your
Lauren

MYSTERY CYCLE

I come in the middle of the January of your life,
holy in this task and rope off space around us.

Like how some molecules huddle in a ring to repel
what's beyond.

You reach for some folded map and catch

my face with the bend of your finger.

What I took from him, what he took from me.
What I took to be chapter 11 was chapter II.
The bag of drugs I found on the ground and took to be a gift.

Beginningless.
We lost our shells years ago.

Behind us are the Futurists
and the double-deck trams.

AFTERWORD

Long after and still,
three horses appear.

I am a child's
corner of that field.
A huge readiness.

I stare into a face with too much

and contain what I don't want to say

and exist so outside my voice
why even talk.

It chills the base of my throat

like some lemon bite too sharp.

Daytime shapes up cool white and blue not
regal enough for you.

The task to touch what exists while we do.
The three horses gone.

NEW YEAR'S EVE DRESS

The New Year's Eve dress makes its wearer
the something to come, the edge of what we know.

There is no satrap with a decree that states nudity is preferred.
There is a river that dictates this to me.

Strapless, thin, short, implying bodies
for warmth, a fireplace, luxury of heat.

I have worn rhinestones.
I have worn Ptolemaic jewelry.

It is winter. I could be in two pairs of socks,
or jeweled, tinseled, sequined in paillettes, lights in darkness.

The future is the 1920s idea of the future.
Tungsten lit. Fritz Lang. *Metropolis.*

So that I could be metallic, sort of tin, the dress I wear
acts as instrument, as fanfare.

I could be the tool you twirl in your hand as it hammers away.

ONLY YOU CAN HEAR THIS

Heavy under the Hudson,

a man climbs out of the new train station crying.

In the escalator's queue, he wipes his face—

in clean, laughterless banality, not offstage.

By and by, he leaves.

He could touch someone.

And if someone touched him,

who is equipped for the answer?

Not me, in the cold of my trench,

boxed up in my own coffers,

back at my desk.

HOT HOUSE ROSES

You can't take the complete person with you.

That's huge, that's everything.

I can't undergo that prevarication in this little leaf dress.

The end of the day, my black spit.

Grave, thinking of it, turning it around until it becomes chatoyant.

Who could figure out a curved ceiling?

Those guys are gone.

I stop by a farm off the highway,

not in color, as I am a place to you,

and you are the dream of the west.

Long rain, neighborly smoke, we keep watching the gold on the pines

for a change with your hand in my hair.

SUNDAY NIGHT BROADCAST

Let's put on a radio show with skipping records
—18th century total harmony—
where a whole section gasps at the same time.

The first sound is one beam
from one mouth.
Even this one-dimensional thing escapes us.

The man I love
loves a virtuoso,
one who can remember and loop in more.

The request comes in,
How I'd love to hear it again, a man says,
so someone hits the button and it plays.

His breath fills the hall,
so many times the size of us.

IN HER STUDY

First love he's all into winter sports and gels his hair and keeps getting in trouble,
keeps watering the yard for the hiss of the hose, loves my twisted braids for waves tonight,
like how in a dispersive prism material dispersion causes color to refract at angles, splitting
white light for a rainbow, or so say my notes atop a cherry desk of personal letters, near a
ring of keys, as I am part-owner of things I can't understand, always drinking diet air, always
finding *real is hunger* in my name, the other anagram, always as in physics, cheerleading,
erect as Nero, I work with normal force (F_n), like a gummi lollipop on a flexible stick,
making my stretch public and out of places to adorn, I've a jewel right in the center
and ribbons like the tail end of regret right before it disappears.

SHÖNE MADONNEN

Like a buck, I walk right into the woods,
listening for the fear into which I was born.

Like a wick burning out more room for itself.

I know the way, but I've no purpose.

My name, the joke, Mountain Man Jack.

By George, by my father,

by winter.

I write down, "tell dad *you're like Homer*."

I used to wear Marlon Brando's *On the Waterfront*
buffalo plaid coat. My brother wore it too.

I'm no hunter,

nothing to raze, no place to sleep.
Tongue-tied trees offer no message how I want, like I want.

To have nothing like this,
twin cherry to being.

IN A FIELD,

you began the second person.

You wore your mother's soft seafoam-green weights for wrists and ankles,

and cold geese flew over their cranberry bog.

Anytime she hurt herself, bumped something, your mother would say *y'mutha.*

In your yard there was a dense smell of the hose

and a farm kitten to whom you fed a meatball.

She wanted to be kept, came back, hid under the barbecue

and seemed to say let me be a painstaking part of this

too much trouble to remove.

The kitten could wrap her paws around your neck,

and the rest of her beat in your hands.

Boundary is a child's word (ducking in parentheses).

Boundlessness hid behind one's ribs (it seemed).

JERSEY SHORE

Didn't meet anyone on the boardwalk though I walked
with a beautiful girl—both of us looking for wet eyelashes,
sweet pleading, a cigarette headache.

All of this motored into one person.

Instead, everyone was tattooed like they paid someone
to stay up with them all night.

All their Hun or Goth bodies.
All the different types of pulse.

My job was to stand right at the front
of the surf store,
my pockets longer than the denim fringe skirt.

I was the crystalline working of a watch.
Hum and tick. Responsive to a very
clear message in a bottle, now lost.

I'll tell you everything we heard:

Soften what you say.
Snake into, instead—

don't speak directly.

Your voice needs
to be defanged—
approach from the side,
don't be too much,

so, like.

Outside, the sky inverted with an unhinged beauty and we

radiated out in rings.

STATE FAIR

I believe in the game
and win the Tamagotchi.

In my hand, it has a pulse or a beat, sort of alive.
I feed it lollipops, jelly hearts. It moves

like a diaphanous creature, like
a complicated multicellular organism,

an extension of me. Against the wall
of the Gravitron, I keep one leg down,

one leg held in a standing split. Mass up,
velocity down, relative rates

at which the constant pressure
holds me in place. It's childish

and deserves a blue ribbon.
I am scared of the ones that spin,

the rides that sling you inside yourself,
the pirate ship held aloft by a cable

that shifts in two directions so
you're falling both ways.

the hammer, its required strength,
asks *are you external?*

Do you really only exist here?
Saved nowhere else.

Sun sets. Look twice nothing's
there. I stand in line as if I were tall.

Lick the side of a lemonade for
water, to say I swallow nothing.

But there it is, that hot metal horse under me,
that ride I pay for, that circle

I make heavy. In gymnastics, all
kinetic potential, I run a full length

of the floor and then stop right before.
My body keeps going,

my skin burns the mats from forehead
to ankle, broken vessels. I ate dirt,

we said. All that rugburn. I had stopped myself
from being thrown across the room. It came out anyway.

"DIADEMS—DROP—"

The place has carved out my sleep. I walk it every night.

On moving here, there were old sounds,
a sputtering meter at the end of a cab ride,

or the back of the ferry, its engine like the
low-end keys of a baby grand,

like a whale, centuries away.

Then too I believed the beauty of things I didn't have,

an evening shrug, light blue, dark red stained-glass windows, staged
and elaborate.

The noun <<cicatrice>>
that sounds more like it,

the citron glow of a scar, still there, the sour of the word,

the softness of the word ruins, the softness of inward ruins,

my signature.

We still measure how long we will live.

A sweetened charge of color
if you unfocus.

But I could lengthen always into this.

THANKSGIVING IN KEY WEST

I want the gas station butter cake
the American girls choose, then bring with them back into their cars.

Hurt. I want familiar people,
but who's familiar enough?

We are quiet. In my lap,
some imported incense.

We have not been invited to anyone's dinner.

I feed my friend chips and salsa
as we drive over the longest bridge in America
to get there,

the Cracked Conch Cafe.
It is rainy, bread and butter still coming.

We stand around
in the center of the diner when I do not mean to

but pour black coffee
on my jean shorts,

a shock to feel the first spill.
We take the cup and leave.

I want this life, this body.
Put me to work.

Put me in the window,
like the thousand flower honey.

GREENERY

Outside,
the neighbor's pinned sheet moves
like a human on the other side of the fence.
Outside my life, I kept saying, to make up for the
shame of doing it wrong. My life, not how it will be,
every wrap around me someone's, to be inside, more.
Outside no sound but the wind I love, sun on my bare foot.
Waiting for everyone to wake up. Here we are, changed, it's
the summer we wanted. A look we planned. We ordered burgers,
and after a question I screamed my laugh you can't take anywhere.
Outside all that is here to hurt us. Outside letting. How can I thank you?
I carried the art over a floor of vents that shot up my dress, blew my hair.
I had expected it. I once asked my parents for a part of my yard. I asked and
if a leaf blew up it meant yes, sideways no. I played in the field a game by myself.
I had to take care of the corn stalks, pigs, myself, that I had no one, that was the game.

EXAPTATION

My doll had an exoskeleton
one could remove like a dress.

Inside, a baby with a ponytail and bow.

That doll had a thorax, it was easy.
You removed half of her,
a kind of leaf,

and there a bodied thing inside,
still in the process of speciating,
a vintage Barbie. It held medieval weight.

At the party, I walked in
as our childhood's doll,

a pioneer in river boots,
Kirsten, the American Girl,
but as St. Lucia, a crown of ivy

unlit, flammable,

until I stood in that fire,

like the salt candle I lit to seem elsewhere
called Swedish dream fresh from the sea,

like the snow moon, bright as interior pineapple,
far-flung, shucked from shell.

MEDIEVAL OPTICS

Yet once more, I get it wrong,

staring into a reversed image.

Once I measured correctly

and was valor in a torso, could carry you

and the phalanx of my forebears. Who am I to say consciousness

cannot be divided into lives seen on us.

You don't sit for your own self-portrait.

I am in tune, a book you have yet to take out, a secret I've barely told.

I collapse to a small point. From here,

I can reach through some periscope out to you.

My friend tells me the future will still need the blues,

we'll need to tell time in parallel ways.

We'll need to name a region's cold wind for comfort.

APOSTASY

Wet with your youth,
you called for champagne in the log cabin
and tried not to burn the thing down.

How you stood still to drink it, a Greek bronze,
a flame over a saint's head.
In the woods,

you rowed across Mink Lake to get here.
A boy held your arms back, your ponytail in his fist
like you were a creature who would bite.

Then that last night in your glasses—
as if wearing them out to the bar
counted as staying in—

How you looked at women
who said, "I'm good,"
meaning they were done.

PSYCHOMACHIA

First facts: female and how much I weighed.

First thrill: losing my voice after hours.

From the world's first cities, it was always a woman

telling the future.

First time a man threw a hundred-dollar bill

at me to fix a broken screen, I was already classically trained in this.

After all, the last few pages of any book are blank, a paper moon.

A green leaflet before the book starts and a green leaflet at the end–

First thing I drew were Gibson girls.

I was young as hell, a girl's first ride.

GUILTY

I walked into the bar with a bunch of toughs,
bullies, The Holy Roman Empire.
They knew the ways in which we could be locked in and out.

One of the times, it made me stop, but not before I drank my
self italicized.

*

Before I gave it up,
I let pain reverberate off every brick wall,

as pain will, as it breaks with abstraction.

But solid as a Grecian marble in a mirror,
I'd tongue the bittersweet eyeliner for application.

Hippocrates measured my pulse, an insistent march figure.
A Riviera-thick cat eye.

Vodka-pale.

*

I watched myself do it.

The sound got on me, and I believed anything
that was power.

Please
don't make me a joke,
I asked someone.

THE VERY ONE

And then those spots were charged with cruelty
when I stepped into them again,
between two men arguing over time, and
a coolblue conditional sky, half of glass.
We ignore a river and each other.
Last summer, decimated at every length, everything
was of stone, but with a wooden color—
how could I abandon it?
How the age of the painting webs
from the last point to the edge, the inside
crushed blue of Ingres' gown, the look they gave,
a violet sharp wavelength stretched to the cyclamen red
of my dress, to me.

I WAS BORN TO MAKE YOU HAPPY

Tough in the breakaway pants, the slick umbros, soffes, shinguards,

wrist tape, nalgenes, prewrap headbands, this training

to not let my marble heart roll out of me, but what else?

Under floodlights I found a twenty on the track and put it in my sports bra—

someone had thrown this bill. Someone had to drive me home—

my boyfriend with no working speedometer.

Window down in the cold, his lip rings, smoking, diamond plating his lungs.

His smoke in a beam of projected light. My coral lip.

Back in my room, I found the twenty pulling off my cheer shell, as it was called,

a shell like a tangerine peel thin and bright. *I'm a fool for you,* we sang.

We grabbed at a generation's things,

then were braided by them, pluralized the future.

We learned by going out to watch boys smoke.

All of it signs and symbols in high school art.

CRAZY

We were in the country.

A video store let us in, thirteen. We knew where to find the VHS,
the one we'd traveled to her lake house to see. A compilation
of the worst things you could watch, sorry to say.
You could watch a cow's center sliced so all of its self came out.

One beer for four girls. We said now we have to get naked and run down the road.

We expressed ideas of not sleeping.

I thought, the woods know I want to barrel through.
Imagined a wind, a sea, the moon, a bonfire, a bunch of skeletons with flags of primary colors;
they're raising us up.

The best people I knew were because of homes. Who was beautiful, whose home could I be let in.

The morning of the first day
of sixth grade,

new girl in town, crush from the farm,

I broke a glass of perfume
and didn't make a face because no one was watching.

My mother tongue? Just a leaning into the wrong words, being corrected
and sticking with this instead;

~ as punctuation.

Don't tease, she can't take it,
I want them to stop

saying of me.

THELYPHTHORIC

Yours was the name I used to let others know I was young.

     —After a concert, a virgin is handed a mic and walks
into the noise of things known at the time.
Access Hollywood asks the 13-year-old: Would you do anything
Britney Spears did? Yes, I answer. Do you love Britney Spears? Yes.
If she, say, started a makeup line, would you buy it? If I wore makeup, yes.
But that's not for littler kids. I'm thanked off screen.

It's okay if nothing is beneath that but there they are: the gears beginning.
Littler is not a word, my friends laugh. I am told beauty will fix it.

VANITY

Lord, I have held onto the mechanical bull,

have removed my hoops pacing with that old high,
have presented fat roses in a glass of water,

have taken my father's never touched coin from its glass case and thumbed it.

I used to think the line "I look so good on you"
was "I left some good on you." I sang it wrong as
this was a time before facts, before searching.

I searched for a desk and a mirror
and found
thousands of images of women smiling.

IF I COULD BREAK YOU—

When the singer laughs on the take
from another century, she sounds so cute.

Her laugh says we're wrong
having her stand in for the dead.

My ancestors wrestle in a half-vanished fresco
and blow in "the new direction of Time."

It is front page news.

It says you have even more,
the tests were wrong everything was wrong.

Good God! Preferable, fine.

We now begin.

"CAN'T YOU SEE I'M A FOOL"

I was once in a denim skirt and cowboy hat, spilling milk in a grocery store.

How many songs did I learn to sing I was the fool?

I am a fool. I know I have been a fool—

these are the early future concepts out of which I turned into myself.

Watching *The Invisible Woman* with my mother:

all we knew of her was she was holding brandy

and a cigarette and was naked and invisible.

A blonde nude wherever you were clothed.

What was that time with my thin knowledge, in a catsuit

out in the cold, in which I found myself on the roof

off of which I almost fell, in cheap heels and drunk?

In chilly Italy, I put out my arms and a man filled them with roses—

happy birthday! So long. No coat, just cowboy boots. I would miss my plane home.

It's unspeakable. I'm asking you to speak it.

HEEL STRETCH

I grew up memorizing chants, learned to fast

and wore shoes made for someone else's hand,

for flying. The kick was the costume.

The leg held in a heel stretch an unbroken column.

All of it saying, Look! How hard I am working against this.

Sweated out and sculpted as a water chestnut.

In competition, frowning gained points as did flyers' bobblehead surprise.

The name of an open hand was star, fist facing out: doughnut, facing in: cheerio.

Nationals in my mind like it could change something in me.

I spent college upside down in exorbitant handstand goals.

I am sent some grass

with a note: *Remember we had cheer practice here?*

Right here, where we studied nothing as we'd been taught.

ANTICIPATING

Like the cowboy who drove cattle through the valley
for three months at a time, I was following some heat.
I woke up feeling like I'd burned the place down and
stumbled upon my mother's hunting knife.
He asked *where's my ring?* patting the space
I made curled up—it's on you it's on you.
In this dream it fell off near my body.
Days are warmer. Why am I so dismal?
Back home on the subway, we went faster.
I let him hold me up, a man who put his hand
on my back *so you don't fall.*
Seated, another man squints to read my gold necklace.
He holds out his hand, watches his gold ring.

SOFT INGÉNUE

That's not it—I say when she tries out my name.

Take the way my mother speaks.

A voice that birthed me who *like butta*

erases what's serious with a joke, an accent.

My first syllable gives two vowels two ways.

First say my name as a rage—

ore of her shore. Or you could be this.

Are is another way, perhaps brighter.

You are something, are you not?

My fake ID had me living on Chic Jon Lane.

There it is, missing a signature,

the omitted passage.

I sign my name soft peach.

TOOLS, CURRENCY

Dark with the bar's interior lamps,
the heft of me is elsewhere, my friends are late.

I sit near a sign that says *trash only*

and remember an underwear model who pulled me by my hair
over to him, told me my hair smelled proprietary.

Whole cities in hats,
others too with warm collars, all who swore to wait for me—

have said into my neck, You smell proprietary, pulling my hair at the beer hall
—their jade, shell, and feathers—

pulling me into their Roman arms bruised with weapons.

I thought I was mathematizable, my age, but
the bartender doesn't, says, sorry, you just have one
of those faces.

The bartender asks where I'm from, what country,
to give me a visitor's discount. Here.

Another bar in New York bans women
from saying *literally.*

They arrive. My friend wears his shirt of dragon fruit, banana, papaya, pineapple.

We try out our feelings on taxidermy—
the animal is the glimmer in its eye, I say, though I love a moose
mounted, I know it is wrong.

Over his laughter, no, the animal is in our eyes.

SUN ORANGE

Was it for this we whispered to no one?

Hanging off the back of a Jeep with just my hands?

In California, we sat around a fire and I broke the code. Not written in my crooked hand
could I say what I had found. I tried to keep it from my future self. She of course would know.
Instead, I wrote how

I walked into freezing Lake Tahoe in a bright green bikini and cried underwater.

How well we believed there was a total, larger, and we knew how to grasp it.
Mix me in.

I called today and you were away,
so I leave this at your ear

and crawl out of the subway to the sun,
exhausted, Debussy light.

That beat has to be willed.

THE TEMPTATION OF BAD NEWS

Something coats you, is born into your birth rattle,
birth knell
before it is reintroduced as fear. Maybe not.

More like something remembered unobtrusively.

A frat's secret
handshake. I'd overseen it once and held on.
Or the laugh of a great aunt who'd slap the table
and whose skin, I was told, was also bad,
like mine. Called upon,   ·
I could bring these forth, if needed,
each an apple in my sack, brushing my side.

HEAT DEVIL

To know even less has a weight for me.

I want only what's see through. I started to tell you—

The filmmaker was showing how sad it was to leave

the high drinking halls of stone, the energetic reward,

my gripping onto the grass.

I used to be—freezing in high heels—young.

But like any loved abstraction, it never existed. I want to angle into being,

with fewer belongings, like a party in palm air with silver dots,

rinsed cobblestone. I know, consistency is a weak logic.

So happy there's more.

MORALITY PLAY

A student asked,
when did the gods live?
I licked the answer
and stamped it flat.
They never lived.
An answer
was on her paper,
not during
recorded history.
She looked at me
aslant, as through branches and leaves
after that.

MEDIEVAL MARGINALIA

Two girls drew an anchor on my bicep then licked their work.

They made me a duct tape bikini and I went in,

my face puffy with chlorine and bare

as pink pearl apples.

Playing cowboy pool, I stayed with myself and hovered right there.

I had such news to deliver. I covered the envelope with stamps

and padded it thick with lined paper. I kept a heartbeat.

ERROR OF THE INGÉNUE

Let me in I said and banged at the piano,
banged at the mesh swing door
because I saw a way in.

Some light opened a man's chest,
no not him, not him.

It followed, if I got it right, I would receive something
larger than the visible returns. The terms would change.

In college, I let a stranger carry me home. He said it wasn't safe.
Said someone could pick me up and take me elsewhere.

The softest part of my head dipped.
Collar bones up. I let him carry me.

Once in the meatpacking district, in the middle of a wide alley,
a man started shaking

when I appeared
he opened his wallet, his zipper,

take everything I have,
he said, just don't hurt me.

BRUTE

Are only the eras we photographed
going to be repeated?
Refine that image, so glaciers remain.
A rushed experience now it is.
Posted and known now it is
not governed. That system has failed, lost-in-the-mall.
I can close my eyes to get home.
If only. Tossing pears to the hogs, tossing
pears he stole, Augustine loved the bad in him.
I want to flip this table here. I want to go down
the very center straight in these heels hah!
Want to divide Atlantic City in this
foodcourt. Of the great storms of me,
one was this weekend. Unbridled firehose.
Don't say a word to me about virtue. I'll start a fight,
take it around the block, undercut in gloves,
answer the phone with a laugh.
I used to hate text as a verb.
It was a childhood boyfriend who taught me
how to select all. Raised on a fast pencil, a sound expiring.

MEDIEVAL MESSENGERS

Like sharing your screen—the feel of someone else's cursor—

a sense you aren't alone in your body. That's how I understood God.

But if we could get proof, we'd have proof.

As a kid, if I thought of my farm kitten Cleo while on my bed

she would come running from another corner of the house.

I keep sending my dad and brother a picture of us on a tractor together.

I always liked that, dad says. I like it too, we say,

the babies on the hay bales.

CHARACTER

When it means the you left on others.

When I told myself keep it up keep it up, like I did when I had with me

my machete and cut bamboo twenty feet and carried it down a mountain.

When it means what I'm claiming mine.

When I leaned one arm against the wall
and made of my body
a velvet draped curtain fifty feet high.

My grandkids will say grandma oh grandma.

I send it out.
Smoke to the lowercase parts of me.
I share her blunt.

What is it about you, the thing around you that is so big

You do not know it.

SIX WINTERS

It's night now, me and this deer in my arms.
Lord knows I won't find my way back easy.

A glowing piano all night
and his pine scented wrist like rain down fat cones.
An aged lawlessness.

He is alone with you before the curtain rises—

I was twirling my hot-tempered telephone
while the man I love held a shirt to his face to hear me breathe.

Full face and the o of her flashlight,
a long exposure in single degrees.

You knew I was alone.
Just a bad penny.

SOBRIETAS

At the gallery opening, a photographer laughs at me and my beer,

his large camera an inch from my cheek, the bulb going off,
a shot of me tilting, bottle in mouth.

I meant to be the present tense handful
in a tang orange dress, melon colored electro.

What would you be like? I showed him.
It would be like this: bare in nectarine, the sustained note of take-off.

What have I offered?
I thought: lift and promise, want with an interior, want in velvet bags,
wine poured in our mouths from a height.

I was more octopus than upright, though, a neon bulb for a heart.

THE IDEA OF LOGGING OFF IS DONE

No more skills of map reading, roomier without them.
50 million years of programming, what else might I be wrong about?

Another century points up and holds a book, unread,
the arguments of faith are over.

Odd age, to be so removed from action, to feel
time as a muddy organization, the forest seeking its watch face.

Sure, but the image did exactly what I wanted in those days.
My direct gaze to you, a chain link fence and clear blue
offered bowls of American cherries out in the sun.

Again, before another century's white barn. Again, on a
brown cordovan couch, a kind of soft leather, on which,
in the late night, I unzipped and stepped through.

WHAT IS THE KNOCKING?

Wisemen and their golden jugs walk on sand through the night
to find this with one hand.

They whistle and the world whistles back.

Now I know the unseen end in a half phrase—almost—
we *almost almost almost*—its marzipan taste,
close to catastrophe, damaged by a lightning bolt 2,000 years ago.
Almost means a near flipping into the other, but it's past.

Over white flowers, amid their inner lives,
(where lately I touched their leaves;)
I slip beneath my belief in objects and am new here
at the black wood desk.

Book, you contain the past.
I want to show you things you once said to me.

There is something you should know:

WHAT IS THE KNOCKING AT THE DOOR IN THE NIGHT?

A doorman claims my old college dorm did not exist.

I say, *it was right here!*
in my ghost uniform.

Back when I would carry a fake old map of the sailor bars by the wharf.

Like a ghost walking down the street, I put a lid on the top of me
and keep looking down.

On the edge of my lip, suddenly a face without needs.
In the warm wind, the stick and attachment of pine,
there is still all that exists against proof that it does.
A field seamed in fog.

NO, NO,

Two leafy crowns, abandoned, hang off a branch in lower Manhattan.
You and your friend have been drinking all day.

You find them—you get the laurel wreaths.
And you wear them out to lunch then into the night.

You are asked if you are ancients, in earnest,
then told to stop laughing, shushed to keep quiet the bar for monks.

You and your friend eat French fries for free.
Dressed for the weather, there's an emerald scent in your ivory frock.

You wear a chain soft as a fish on collarbones, your summer neck,
the metal links in water weight.

The holy kingdom is said to have shot through a room of strangers.
The gold-ground healing kings. Remember them?

Discovering silence in every place you could—
as a kid what were you seeking?

THREE STRANGE ANGELS

Awed at something off to the right,
across the meadow

I walked through
and back

to the fern yards of cabins where men have
stomped their boots. Men who drop

to their knees as they've done.
How about no more languid draping of myself

on a chest, hurtless
in the cabin's heady scent.

The fireplace responds with mutterings
from years and erased names.

Lord I love a cicada year, the smell of a stone room.

You're home.

I write it down and keep nothing around it.
Like the chestnuts too hot in my hands cracked by a kind artist.

ADMIT THEM, ADMIT THEM

Those days I knew I had to listen for you.
I used the simple present everywhere,
let a plant grow a shoot to touch my pillow.
It grew full of reaching.
What I knew was conclusion,
it hollowed me to be a louder bell,
it taught my mouth how to keep and take time.
But I couldn't stop standing over you, the source of the pulse.

This is the last heat
of my bachelor days in the lonely hunting cabin.
I speak to you on an ancient telephone where I am the vault.
For a blanket, I place my parka on the sun dry grass,
my tight black jeans get hot.
Everything I have is yours, I tell the circle
in the woods.

PALINODE

Out here,
the artist adjusts
his light. It feels like
a beach house in NJ,
an outdoor shower,
wet stones, crabs for dinner.
Seventy degrees, the internet is down.
No one has ever heard this song,
we are only getting what's left,
they say on the old radio.
On the recording, someone shouts, *here we go!*
Someone talks on the take.
I want to remind you
of what will be easier.
Everything can be
true.

FOX

Beneath the earth there is a strip of magma from me to you.
This place hasn't changed much in 200 million years.

It still smells like geese in vees, grass under melting snow, muddy boots.

In the font of everyone I know is how I read you, how I talk with you.
We create the instrument of a sound we want to hear

and make it say: I am not going to hurt you.
The last day of winter, Veronica Lake in a white collared shirt.

I stamp my signet ring into wax.
The message calls itself a lake, caws itself to smallness.

And I challenge something in you to be lonely.

THE BIRTHDAY CONCERT

It's a miracle it survives, someone says of the fuzzy recording over the radio.
And it's the truth.
It happens again.

The sole oboe in the center like pulling a needle from muscle,
like one with a lantern going back and forth.

I let him touch both parts of my name

and everything came forward.
I showed him I was a prize fighter in the ring.
Gave him three bucks and he gave me 50 cents back.
What a joke.

But when the sun shone blue in the high window,
wind in clouds, wood painted white—
the hands of no language could wrap me.

It's better when you are listening with someone.

It's best when I'm listening with you, the radio says to me and anyone
who will listen.

DOUBLE PORTRAIT

It's her,

my father says,

of his mother,
but to some extent it's me, I'm the echo.

Vines of shit grow around you—
he shapes his hands like the marble
of a god fighting—*and that is you,*

what holds the thing together.

A bow that snapped with time?

We zoom in at the expense of the whole,
to see a garnet in silver,
a color that stays.

THE ORACLE

These dusty suede shoes,
their unsure angle
up the staircase by the live oaks,

the fountain on repeat, blinking, closing off the sun,
the air for walls, of which I could lean right out.

Rain pricks my legs, my forest sweater,
this vegetable garden lit with sprinklers.

Peacock-eyed and baroque.

Suspend this question.
It's now isn't it.

WANDERJAHRE

I taste the mint off a stem and stomp around the field. I do this every day.
Near the road, I pass the pigs in the back of the pickup, all of us squinting.

Into its animal, June. My lazy fire all night.
When I return to New York, I walk the museum's basement,
dark but for the mini lights of the carpeted theater, my bachelor's journey.

What is a husband? When with a running start I can hold my whole self,
jump the length of the room. When with eyes closed at a party,
we can all brush them off the table, pile them into our laps. I am bad.
I walk around amazed.

THE STONE BRUISE

Sharp-set, I rose,
asked *Let today be my last day*
as nude kitchen cat,

so much time in there
drinking coffee from lilac bowls.

Time to go.

I used to mean to live here.

Now the subway
I have waited for, petted its side.

I scoff as if I've tamed it
here in two braids,
in clasped suspenders, violin brown.

Seated in the subway,
Dionysus reaches down
to brush something off my cheek
as if his own or a child's

before we see you.

The last time, I had a gauzy air, the thousand nudes like static—
if I touched your name you answered me.

I arrive at the party with coral tulips.

It is easy

mistaking a painting for a candle, a flash for a flare,
rolling around in a rented room, trouble-limbed.

I am ready if you are.
I tap you to incorporate me.

THE BOWER

I curved

and let his big hand fall between my arms and legs.

He woke and touched the bed, where did I leave you?

Asleep, I walked the grounds.

Later, I eyed myself alone with her cards,

like a fire burning

in sensory neglect.

I couldn't even

speak on burger night. I scared myself nameless.

I walk through it,

a wet field in secret,

jealous of myself.

THE BUTTERFLY MUSEUM

Reason predicts lapses in reason,
and logic has a weighted right answer.

The idea is to get as many on us as possible.
The butterflies.

They do not land—
We have been crying and they can tell.

You know what you kind of look like? my friend asks me.
Know when you put sunglasses on babies?

We kick around abandoned yellow flower heads,
decaying palm fronds.

I am sickened by their food,
a bowl of sugar water,
the forked fruits.

Sweating in mint shorts with swans,

and a flower in water
like the opening of a folded note,

backbend of petals,

kind to other travelers.

THE FIRST SILENCE

You knew I could close myself
around someone like that.

The only man who can part a crowd and pull me
by the belt.

Mid-morning smoothest,
his choice a satin leaf,

yellow strawberry guava.

Constancy is a word slow as it sounds,
with as many delays?

Antique brass is the seat of years' trust.

You crest a tongue to my brass heart.

Marry me tonight,

I'm trying to say.

LOWLINESS

I have hurt women. They have handed it back.
We have both been the idling space.
We have embedded in language mistakes.

I'm far from the things I knew and wrestle to a win.

I imagine you locked in the verse and chorus of your own.

You were like the typo carved in stone at the Lincoln Memorial—the Euture, Eu, still good.

You've the bandleader's power. You can enter.

Illusions got named after us.

Near the post office, I found a free newspaper, read it, it was like that.

Or, what does not properly belong to me, I take for reality.

I longed for someone to bushwhack through space to get to me.

You think forgiveness is inherently selfish.

The envoy reminds us of what we have done.
Remember every bar with a passcode?
Something changed in the course of reading this.

SURE EXCEPT DON'T

Champagne listing
around to each holiday

holding my friend's smoky hands
like the last lick of flame,

a scent of seated tigers,
too sweet gold.

We were taught to bite
our initials in a sailor's neck

while another wedding
processional passed by

in a private language.
Though I never anesthetized

the right part,
I am still sad to end this.

The advice I gave then ended:
"—you bet."

NJ TRANSIT

The streetlight on the maroon of my sweatshirt is glowing my pages red.
Train's here.

I'm still getting emails about Sinatra Day from the old library

as if somehow I am still in the Dairy Queen parking lot
as if they need to reach my grandmother swimming in the Passaic River
as if they found out we got locked in the movie theater after its last showing of *Josie and the Pussycats*.

How tired I'd be
from the switch of jumps and the tooth of the weave,
attempting gymnastics on my old trampoline.
I can't compensate now without a running start,
without my brain looping off some effort to the air.

How tired I'd be
from the weight of the trees but I was light enough then.

"THANK YOU"

He says to himself or the air
for the memory coming back to him.
He wants to remember the last time he was in an old jazz club.
The oldest? This one sure is, where he is right now.
An upright bass. A strawberry on his plate, misspent, happy.
Everyone in the room becomes a jelly, all of you,
and each of us gets to ignore this for another time.
Better than this one? No just as.

THE WAKE

You're to be at mine or
I'm to be at yours.

You're going to have to choose a fig,
pour seltzer in a clear plastic cup.

You'll have to hear my life,
condensed in a way that it takes the center out of you,

so you topple, in a way that makes
the sky, your mouth, open.

In the way a horse thief will take your life,
I'll have to address those who've been touched—

they will be unbelievably gentle about you.
To imagine that a thief will reach your life,

I imagine myself an old gentleman with my round gold glasses.
And if I'm the old gentleman,

I am not yet the strange breeze waving your ringlet
and the ivied trunk.

I will treat the affected ones,
I'm going to deal with them

missing you, unbound, looking for the way he went,
that thief who hit your life and with it went.

I will have to talk to those who touched you too.
Oh, one will say.

You will have to talk to those who touched me,
my every shipboard romance.

You will have to choose a figure
pour the coriander into a container that is transparent,
dark citron, emerald never.

You must hear my life.

GAME KING

Atlantic City

Every machine's song plays at once—

roulette, gold pays, I heart jackpots, wicked winnings.

Fortuna goddess of luck says

if you want ten wishes you can have them,

you don't have to be rough about it.

You found the oracle or the gift store and have asked for

- Parsimony
- a newsworthy dream
- *The Big Sleep* by yourself
- again the lights and umbrellas under all the rainy windows you've ever known
- a diamond for Delmore Schwartz
- a bright night's hedge maze
- a heaven-born show-off
- a beat for a humble fan of vogue
- to address the messenger
- if I could keep you in the circle

Quick strike,
you won.

As burlily undoes itself, burr unto lily.

LOST POEM

There's a typo we'd never see today, an upside-down letter
pulled from the type drawer.

And a sound you'll surely never hear again in earnest:
childhood's slammed door

signifying the one you love has signed off.
I once declared,

I'm as high up on his buddy list as possible
and it meant I spent all day on the phone with you,

a soft interior car feeling,
velvet ribbons, cream and olive.

Extinct is the understanding
of the feeling of the phrase, *he wrote on my wall.*

And extinct allowing one at a cafe to lean in and give a prophecy.
What was that chaotic ease in those years, where an angel could pass through.

I remember their gauging
if they could lean over my thin paged book to let me know.

I remember their expression like
a room of windows near City Hall.

The expression like a bivalve
you may want to open

as if there was another girl inside.

THE HISTORICAL RECORD

The man can't tell if the marks are his daughter's or his father's.
Where is his father? Which is his hand?
Whose notes are on the printed text, an art history book,
one he bought and she stole. 664 pages of men.
Written the year of my father's birth.
We accrue meaning with the repetition of each year.
There are cases that prove otherwise, I know that now,
but for an age, my blood combed it through my body
in a coded exchange.
But logic has never changed. Like a string
of Greek music from the second century,
it is bright and sweet.
We keep passing it down and testing you.
My grandfather's art history book was held

under basement lights.   We all have the same mouth, absorbed
in growth, empty nights.   Not a single watch hand where I live.

RIGHT HERE IN TOWN

The librarian was trying to tell me that fear exists even after we're dead.
The ghosts in the corner there, the way a certain beast wants a dark hole.
What shelters. They've built an addition so the ghosts will leave.

I'd rather walk around than hide in a weird corner,
bat a glass off a table, be an imp.

They need what's comforting, he said.

These may be true statements, but we have no way out from the question stem.

Today was so bright, it's fall.
You can wear whatever the hell you want.

Let's snap into ourselves.

The closest I've gotten would be in all this silence.
I assume it can be done one way, without any armor,
like how we used our arms and adamancy and

Something opened up.

NOTES

The titles and phrases below are borrowed lines, lyrics, and song titles:

"Diadems—drop—" is Emily Dickinson.

"Guilty," "I was born to make you happy," "Crazy," "Can't you see I'm a fool," "Anticipating," and "I look so good on you" are Britney Spears ("Fool" is Shakira as well).

"If I could break you" is H.D.

"Six Winters" is Tomas Tranströmer.

"What is the knocking?," "What is the knocking at the door in the night?," "No, no," "Three strange angels," "Admit them, admit them," and "the new direction of Time" are D.H. Lawrence.

ACKNOWLEDGMENTS

Thank you to the hardworking editors of the following publications for giving homes to poems in this book:

8 Poems, Allium, A Journal of Poetry & Prose, American Poetry Journal, Bennington Review, Biscuit Hill, Blackbird, Bloodroot Literary Magazine, Bodega Magazine, BOMB, Chicago Review, The Common, Hampden-Sydney Poetry Review, Hotel Amerika, jubilat, The Literary Review, Normal School, Pine Hills Review, Pleiades, Poetry Northwest, Poetry Online, Post Road, Sixth Finch, SWWIM, The Threepenny Review, Tupelo Quarterly, West Branch, What Rough Beast, Yuzu Press

To the incredible Poetry Northwest editors: Kevin Craft, Abi Pollokoff, Brittany Amborn, and every member of the team, thank you so much for your belief in my work, for bringing this book into the world, and for all the ways in which you have offered your generosity and kindness. Thank you to Kary Wayson for sharing your brilliance with me and these pages.

Thank you to the Hambidge Center for the Creative Arts and Sciences where much of this book was formed. Thank you, Thomas Steinborn and everyone at FRIEDA, eternally grateful for the workshops, conversation, new ideas, and connection.

Thank you to Jesse Hedges, my home. Artists and friends who have my whole heart, Adrianna de Svastich, Annabel Graham, Caitlin Wells, Chase Berggrun, Chelsea Bieker, Grant Miller, Jack Papanier, Justine Champine, Kay Cosgrove, Kayleb Rae Candrilli, Kat Fayerweather, Katelyn Van Schaik, Lindsey Sosin, Marcus Jade, Matthew Lane, Megan Duffy, Molly Tolsky, Omotara James, Rachel Morgese, Tochukwu Okafor, Tony Y. Fu, Varun Mehra, and my *No Tokens* family—I love you!

My admiration and gratitude for early readers of these poems. Hannah Beresford, for being my better poetry half. Stephen Hilger, for your brains, perception, and laugh. T Kira Māhealani Madden, ever in awe of your sharp insight and goodness. Dionissios Kollias, thank you for reading every page, seconds old, wherever you were in the world. Talking about poetry with you has taught me how much there is still to learn. My most sincere and humble thanks to my family for your expansive love and support.

Lauren Hilger is the author of *Lady Be Good* (CCM, 2016). Named a Nadya Aisenberg Fellow in poetry from MacDowell, she has also received fellowships from the Hambidge Center and the Virginia Center for the Creative Arts. Her work has appeared in *BOMB*, *Harvard Review*, *Kenyon Review*, *Pleiades*, *The Threepenny Review*, *West Branch*, and elsewhere. She serves as a poetry editor for *No Tokens*.

POSSESSION SOUND POETRY SERIES

Sierra Nelson, *The Lachrymose Report*
Lauren Hilger, *Morality Play*

Poem text set in Bodoni with
titles in Source Sans Variable
Book design by Abi Pollokoff
Printed on archival quality paper

Poetry NW Editions is an independent,
non-profit educational press in residence
at Everett Community College.

Founding Editor: Kevin Craft
Managing Editor: Abi Pollokoff

CPSIA information can be obtained
at www.ICGtesting.com
Printed in the USA
BVHW052243220223
659053BV00002B/11

9 781949 166057